WAR MACHINES

ARTILLERY

Simon Adams

W
FRANKLIN WATTS
LONDON • SYDNEY

IN ASSOCIATION WITH

IMPERIAL WAR MUSEUM

First published in 2007 by Franklin Watts

Franklin Watts
338 Euston Road
London NW1 3BH

Franklin Watts Australia
Level 17/207 Kent Street
Sydney, NSW 2000

A CIP catalogue record for this book is available from the British Library.

Dewey number: 623.4'1

ISBN 978 0 7496 7171 6

Printed in China

Franklin Watts is a division of Hachette Children's Books, an Hachette Livre UK company.

Editor: Sarah Ridley
Editor-in-chief: John Miles
Designer: Jason Billin
Art director: Jonathan Hair

A note on sources used for this book: The specifications and statistics in this book are compiled from various sources and amended to include information held by the Imperial War Museum.

Picture credits: All images copyright © Imperial War Museum. Cover t Q1294, bl Q831, bm Q108354, br BU10500; title page main MH 12968, bg STT7640; pp 4-5 bg Q58198, p4 MH7739, p5 Q65800; pp 6-7 bg Q70443, p6 Q70236, Q23801; p8 Q564, p9t Q917, 9b Q831; pp10-11 bg Q7269, p 10 Q1294, p11 Q6460; p12 Q23858, p13t Q23873, p13b Q23959; pp14-15bg Q65799Q, p14 Q65802, p15 Q65800; p16 Q108354, p17 Q58198; pp18-19bg B6308, p18 B6004, p19t B10383, p19b B12607; pp20-21bg MH7826, p20t STT7640, p20b MH7739, p21t E7049, p21b MH7759; pp22-23bg MH12991, p22 MH12966, p23 MH12968;pp24-25bg EA73801, p24 EA73796, p25t EA73786, p25b EA73849; pp26-27bg MH862, p26 MH869, p27 MH861; p 28 CL3407, p29 BU10500; p30-31bg MH7826.

Contents

Introduction

Artillery is the class of heavyweight guns that are pulled by horses or armoured vehicles, as opposed to light guns, such as rifles or machine guns, that can be carried by hand.

Classification

There are two main types of artillery: guns, which fire high-speed shells at a lower trajectory (flight path), and howitzers, which lob heavier, slower shells at a higher trajectory. Artillery is described by its weight: field or light, medium and heavy. Field or light guns can be towed from place to place but heavy guns are difficult to move, need assembling in position, and are slow to fire.

Types of shell

There are many types of shell fired by artillery. High-explosive shells are packed with explosives; they blow up when they hit their target. A shrapnel shell is packed with shrapnel, usually metal balls, and has a bursting charge that explodes in flight, showering the enemy with metal. Armour-piercing shells have a dense core to penetrate the armour of enemy tanks.

Calibre

Artillery is also classified by the internal calibre of its gun barrel: a 75 mm gun has a calibre of 75 mm. Confusingly, different countries employ different systems, as the Germans and French have always used metric measurements, while the British used to use imperial ones. They now use metric. Even more confusingly, the British have also described their artillery by the weight of its shell, so a 60 pounder medium howitzer was fighting alongside a 9.2 inch heavy howitzer during the First World War.

All the artillery in this book saw action in either the First World War (1914–18) or the Second World War (1939–45).

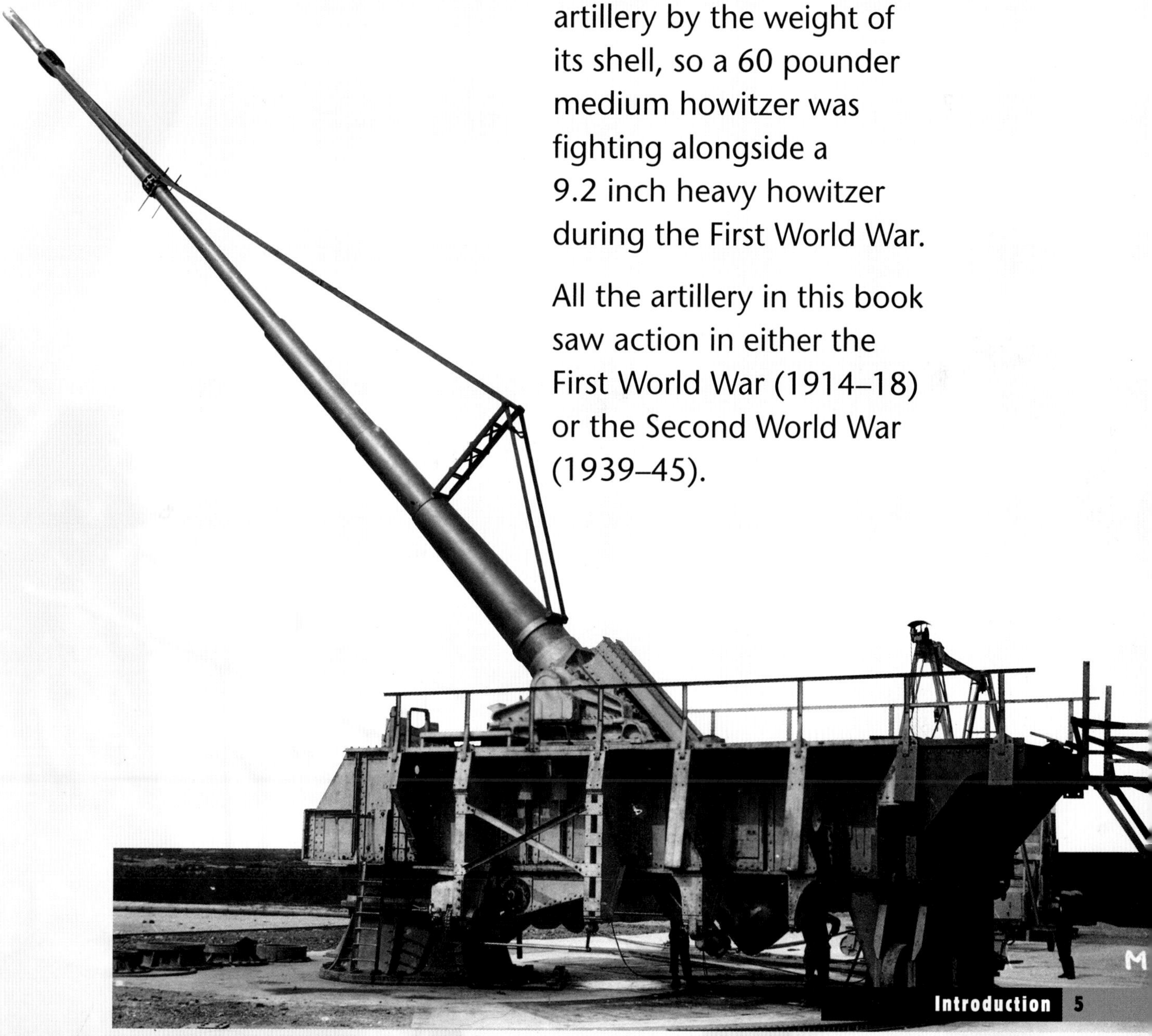

Model 1897 75 mm Field Gun

The French 75, as it was commonly called, was the most famous field gun of the First World War. The gun was designed between 1891 and 1896 and went into production in 1897.

Long service

By the outbreak of war in 1914, more than 4,000 French 75s were in service. The French continued to use this model until the fall of France to the Germans in 1940, ten months after the start of the Second World War.

SPECS & STATS

Crew	6
Total weight	1,190 kg (2,620 lb)
Barrel length	2.72 m (8.9 ft)
Carriage	6 horses, or artillery tractor

▼ *The versatile '75' was even used as a mobile anti-aircraft gun. Mounted on a lorry, it was easily movable.*

FACT FILE

- ★ The gun's hydro-pneumatic recoil mechanism and wheel brakes kept it stable when firing, which meant that the gun did not have to be repositioned before it fired the next shell. It thus achieved a rapid and accurate rate of fire.
- ★ The quick-acting breech mechanism (for reloading) meant that the gun could fire more than 20 shells a minute.

▲ *This French 75 was well camouflaged to hide it from enemy gunners.*

Battle triumphs

The light and mobile French 75 distinguished itself in two main battles. At the Battle of the Marne in 1914 it helped to stop the invading German army from reaching Paris. Two years later, during the lengthy battle for the city of Verdun in 1916, 1,000 French 75s were in action day and night, firing more than 16 million shells. However, although the gun was good against infantry, it was not powerful enough against heavily defended positions, and it was gradually replaced by heavier field artillery.

ARMAMENTS

Calibre	75 mm (3 in)
Weight and type of shell	5.2 kg (11.7 lb) high-explosive shell 7.2 kg (16 lb) shrapnel shell
Muzzle velocity	529 m/second (1,735 ft/second)
Range	9,000 m (9,850 yd)
Rate of fire	15–30 rounds/minute

60 pounder Mk I
Medium Howitzer

The 60 pounder (pdr) was the main medium howitzer used by the British during the First World War.

It was most effective at knocking out enemy batteries, as it had a long range and fired its heavy shells with great accuracy. However, its rate of fire – two rounds per minute – was slow.

▼ *The gun crew stood well back when firing took place.*

FACT FILE

★ A Mk II version of 1918 was more powerful but also 1,000 kg (2,200 lb) heavier. This meant that it could only be towed by a caterpillar tractor or manoeuvred on fixed rails.

SPECS & STATS

Crew	8
Total weight	4,470 kg (4.4 tons)
Barrel length	4.3 m (14 ft)
Carriage	12 horses

▲ *A team of horses was required to move a 60 pounder into position.*

Service history

The 60 pounder Mk I was designed in 1904 and saw extensive service on the Western Front during the First World War. Both this and the Mk II version continued in service with the British army into the Second World War, the last ones seeing action in North Africa between 1940 and 1943.

▼ *A battery of 60 pounders in position on the Western Front.*

ARMAMENTS

Calibre	12.7 cm (5 in)
Weight and type of shell	27 kg (60 lb) high explosive, shrapnel or gas
Muzzle velocity	640 m/sec (2,080 ft/sec)
Range	11,353 m (12,300 yd)
Rate of fire	2 rounds/minute

9.2 in Mk I
Heavy Siege Howitzer

The British 9.2 inch (in) heavy siege howitzer came into service in July 1914, just in time for the outbreak of the First World War.

British Expeditionary Force

One of these large guns went across to France in August with the British Expeditionary Force, but it did not see any action until March 1915.

SPECS & STATS

Weight of gun	15,240 kg (15 tons)
Carriage	Three trucks drawn by traction engines or teams of horses

▼ *The crew of the howitzer prepare it for action.*

Jumping gun

The gun was not designed for mobility, as it took 36 hours to assemble or dismantle. Because the gun had a short barrel, it had a tendency to jump when fired. This problem was solved by bolting a box filled with 9,150 kg (9 tons) of earth on to the front of the gun platform.

ARMAMENTS

Calibre	23.4 cm (9.2 in)
Weight and type of shell	132 kg (290 lb) high explosive
Muzzle velocity	368 m/sec (1,197 ft/sec)
Range	9,286 m (10,060 yd)

▼ *Camouflage netting hid the howitzer and its shells.*

FACT FILE

★ The 9.2 in Mk I was originally designed as a siege artillery gun to attack fortresses.

★ The Mk II version, which appeared in 1917, had a longer range of 12,750 m (13,935 yd). This version required an extra 8,345 kg (9 tons) of earth in the box to keep it steady.

The 'Long Max'

The 'Long Max' was a German 38 cm SKL/45 naval gun that was adapted during the First World War for use on land.

Transporting the gun

The gun travelled to its destination on a railway wagon and then was mounted on a turntable in a concrete pit. A steel girder construction built across the pit acted as a mount so that the gun pointed upwards at the correct angle. A narrow-gauge railway trolley transported its large shells.

▼ *This Long Max is well camouflaged to hide it from the enemy.*

SPECS & STATS

Weight of gun	73,500 kg (72 tons)
Barrel length	17.1 m (56 ft)
Carriage	Railway wagon, then mounted on a turntable in a concrete pit

ARMAMENTS

Calibre	38 cm (15 in)
Weight of shell	750 kg (1,650 lb)
Muzzle velocity	1,040 m/second (3,412 ft/second)
Range	47.5 km (29.7 miles)
Rate of fire	2.5 rounds/minute

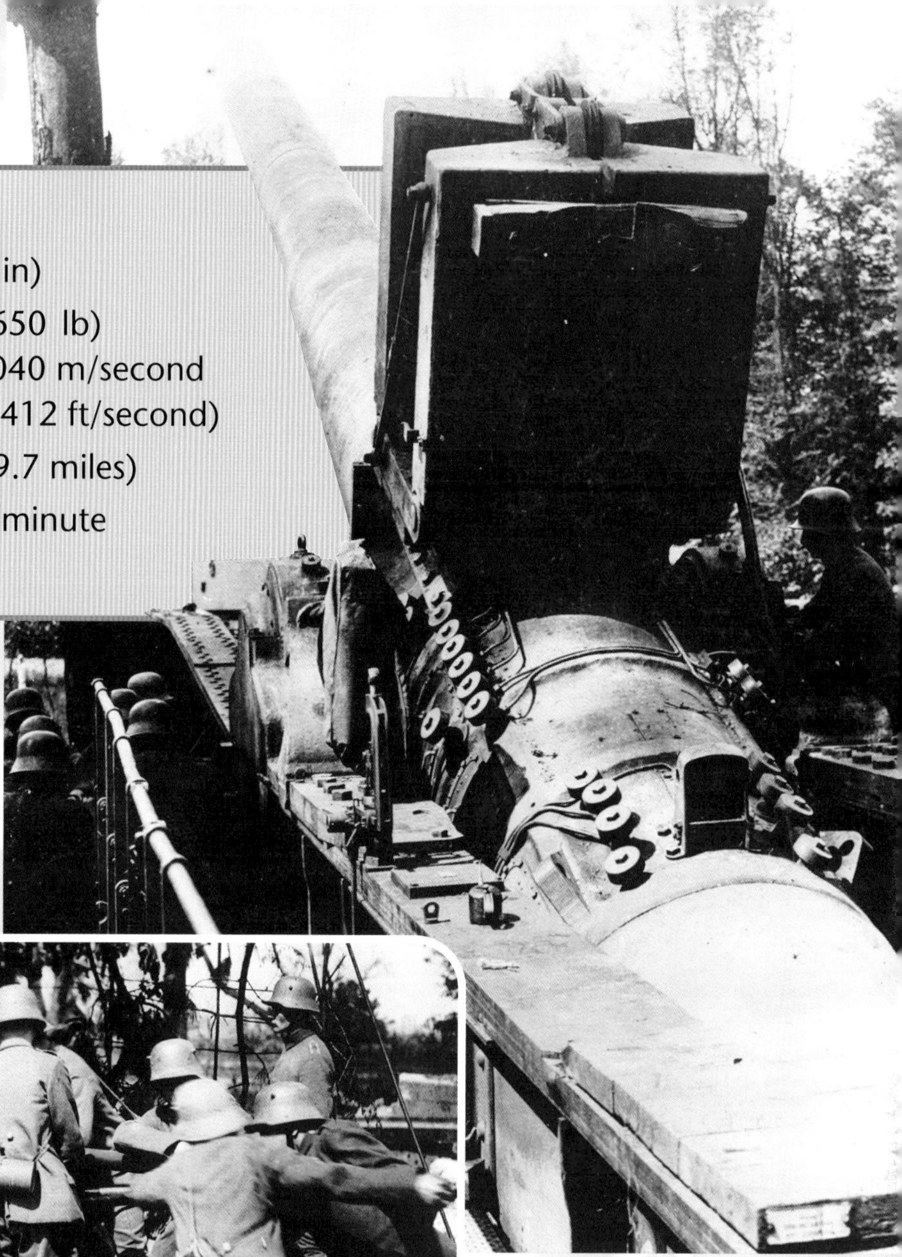

► *Seen from the rear, the Long Max was a vast and complex gun.*

◄ *Heave men – the Long Max is armed for action.*

Long-range gun

The Germans used this gun for long-distance shelling of towns and aerodromes. They installed the first one in eastern France during February 1916 to shell Verdun and its surrounding forts. While these large guns were effective, they were difficult to move around and get ready to fire. As a result, few came into service.

The 'Paris Gun'

At 7.18 am on 21 March 1918, a high-explosive shell landed in Paris.

It had been fired by the Germans from the forest of Courcy, 120 km (75 miles) away, and arrived so quietly that the Parisians thought they had been bombarded by a silent airship. The gun that fired this shell was known as the 'Paris Gun' and its purpose was to bombard Paris.

Huge range

The gun is considered by some historians to have been a terror weapon built by Germany to demoralise the French. Because the gun had such a huge range, its gunners had to take account of the rotation of the Earth when calculating where its shells would land.

FACT FILE

★ Each shell fired by the 'Paris Gun' reached almost five times the speed of sound and reached up into the stratosphere, higher than any other human missile in history until the first successful V-2 test flight in October 1942 (see pages 28-29).

Assembling the Paris Gun at its testing site in Germany.

ARMAMENTS

Calibre	21 cm (8.3 in)
Weight and type of shell	94 kg (210 lb) high explosive shell
Muzzle velocity	1,600 m/sec (5,200 ft/sec)
Range	130 km (80 miles) in 170 seconds at max altitude of 40 km (24 miles)
Rate of fire	1 round/3 minutes

SPECS & STATS

Crew	80 German naval gunners commanded by an admiral
Weight of gun	256 tonnes (252 tons)
Barrel length	28 m (92 ft) with a 6 m (20 ft) smooth bore extension
Carriage	Rotating mount

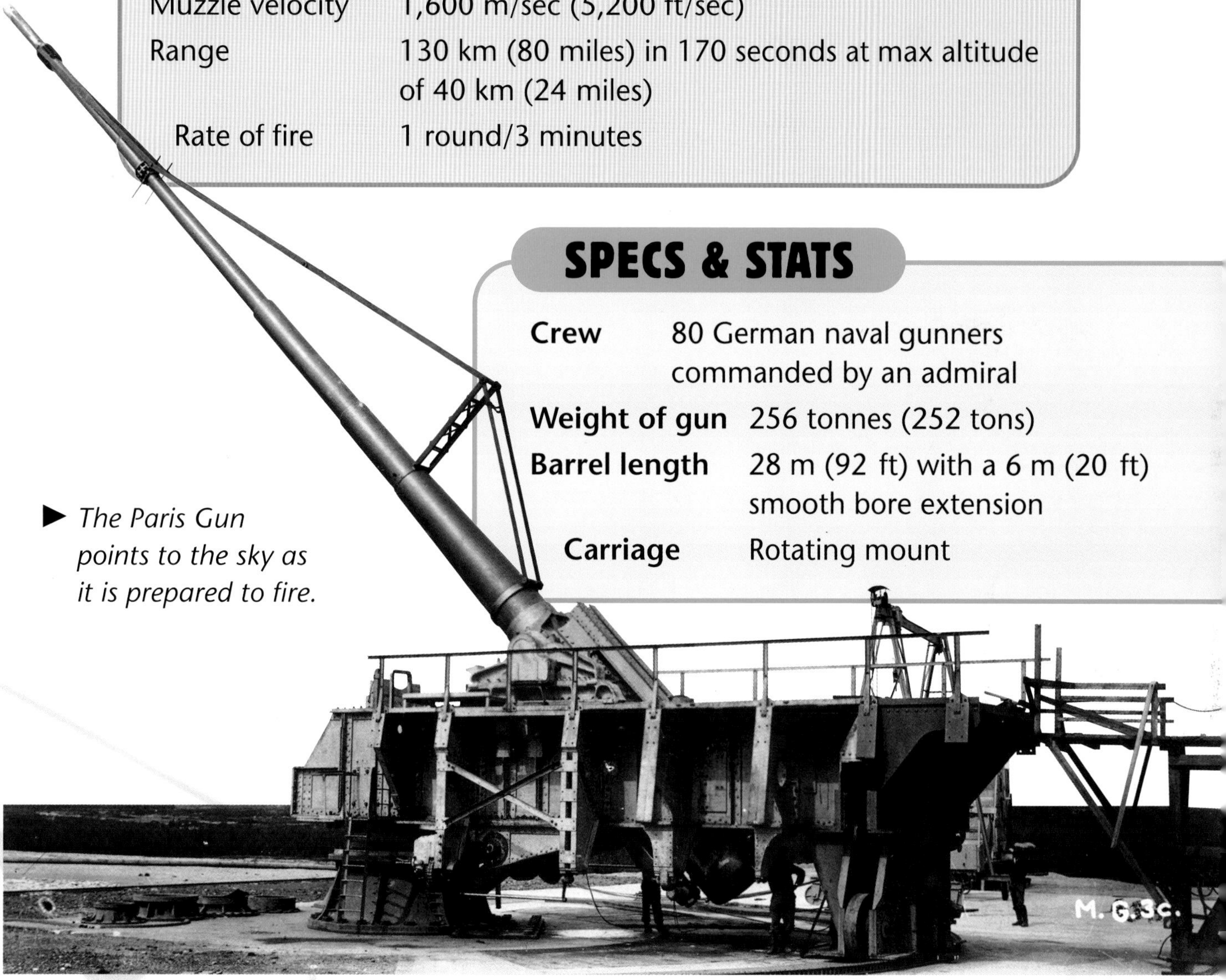

► *The Paris Gun points to the sky as it is prepared to fire.*

Design faults

Its accuracy was not that good: gunners could hit Paris, but not a specific target in the city. The gun was also not that effective, as each shell was fired at such a high speed that it wore away the bore of the gun. After 65 shells had been fired – each one slightly bigger to fit the ever-widening bore – the barrel had to be re-bored.

520 mm Schneider Howitzer

The French 520 mm Schneider howitzer holds first place in the record books for firing the biggest shells of the First World War.

Each shell was 1,420 kg (3,130 lb) in weight and 520 mm (20.5 in) in diameter. The shells were designed to penetrate their target before exploding. The gun came into service in May 1918, but saw little action before the war ended that November.

ARMAMENTS

Calibre	520 mm (20.5 in)
Weight of shell	1,420 kg (3,130 lb)
Range	16 km (10 miles)

▼ *The angle of the howitzer's barrel could be altered up or down, but not traversed side to side.*

FACT FILE

★ Three other Schneider howitzers saw service during the First World War. The 105 mm and 155 mm howitzers were both light field guns, while the 220 m (model 1917) was a heavy artillery gun.

★ The French armaments firm of Schneider was founded by two brothers, Joseph and Adolphe, who took over an old iron foundry in Le Creusot in central France in 1836. The firm still exists today as a manufacturer of electrical instruments.

Mounted on rails

The 520 mm Schneider was fixed on to a railway carriage just under 30 m (100 ft) long which weighed almost 300,000 kg (290 tons). Because it could not traverse, the carriage was towed round a curved siding so that its gun was pointing in the right direction. When it was fired, the recoil was so great that the carriage rolled back down the track.

▼ *Firing the howitzer on its carriage.*

Bofors 40 mm
Light Anti-Aircraft Gun

In 1928 the Swedish navy ordered the development of a new 40 mm naval anti-aircraft gun from the Bofors company.

The gun proved to be light, fast and reliable and a ground-based version on a four-wheeled carriage was soon developed. Seventeen different nations bought the model and it became the most widely used anti-aircraft gun of the Second World War.

British usage

The British army adopted the gun in 1937. Its accuracy and rate of fire were particularly effective against low-flying or dive-bombing aircraft.

▼ *Small and portable, the Bofors was an effective anti-aircraft gun.*

A number of versions were also developed for the Royal Navy. So successful was the gun that it remained in service with the British army until the 1980s.

▲ *The crew of a Bofors gun guard bridges across the Rhine in the last months of the Second World War.*

FACT FILE

★ The Bofors gun could be fired from its carriage with no set-up required, although it was not always that accurate. If the gunners had time, they could use the tow-bar and muzzle lock as levers to raise the wheels off the ground and lower the gun onto supporting pads. Two additional legs folded out on either side. This could be done in less than a minute.

SPECS & STATS

Crew	6
Total weight	1,981 kg (1.95 tons)
Barrel length	2.24 m (7.5 ft)
Carriage	Four-wheeled towable carriage

ARMAMENTS

Calibre	40 mm (1.6 in)
Weight and type of shell	0.9 kg (2 lb) high explosive
Maximum ceiling	7,193 m (23,600 ft)
Muzzle velocity	881 m/second (2,890 ft/second)
Range	7,160 m (23,500 ft)
Rate of fire	120 rounds/minute

► *A gunner finds time to write a Christmas card home.*

5 cm PaK 38
Anti-Tank Gun

▲ *The 5 cm PaK 38 is in the centre, with its successor, the larger 7.5 cm PaK 40, on the left and its predecessor, the smaller 3.7 cm PaK 36 on the right.*

The German 5 cm PaK 38 anti-tank gun was developed in 1938 and entered service in April 1940.

Tungsten shells

When the German army attacked the Soviet Union (USSR) in 1941, they used the PaK 38 gun to fire armour-piercing shells with a core of tungsten, a very hard, heavy metal, at Soviet tanks. These tungsten-cored shells could penetrate 8.6 cm (3.4 in) into armour at a range of around 470 m (1,500 ft), making the gun hugely effective against most tanks. After the supply of tungsten ran out in 1942, the gun's effectiveness using other shells dropped considerably.

◀ *This side view of the gun shows its lightweight construction.*

The low silhouette of the gun made it easy to conceal, which was especially important when fighting in the exposed Western Desert of North Africa.

▲ *British gunners load a shell into a captured PaK.*

FACT FILE

★ PaK stands for *Panzerabwehrkanone*, the German word for 'anti-tank cannon'.

★ The PaK 38 had solid rubber tyres that needed little maintenance and conserved rubber, a scarce commodity in Germany during the war.

SPECS & STATS

Crew	6
Total weight	986 kg (2,174 lb)
Barrel length	3 m (9.85 ft)
Carriage	Split-trail (two-pronged) carriage on two wheels

ARMAMENTS

Calibre	5 cm (1.97 in)
Weight and type of shell	2.8 kg (6.2 lb) A-P shell
Muzzle velocity	835 m/second (2,740 ft/second)
Range	2,745 m (9,000 ft)
Rate of fire	13 rounds/minute

◀ *A close-up of the breech.*

5.5 in Mk III Medium Gun

The British 5.5 inch (in) medium gun first entered service in the Western Desert in North Africa against the Germans and the Italians in May 1942.

Its carriage and breech mechanisms were not adequate at first, and it had a disappointing range. However, various design changes and a lighter shell soon made it highly effective.

Long service

The Mk III gun soon became one of the most effective guns in the British army and saw action in almost every theatre of war. It remained in service until 1978.

The split-tail carriage of the gun is opened out to stabilise it during firing. Note the open breech.

ARMAMENTS

Calibre	14 cm (5.5 in)
Weight and type of shell	45.5 kg (100 lb) high-explosive shell, later reduced to a 36 kg (80 lb) shell
Muzzle velocity	517 m/second (1,700 ft/second)
Range	14 km (8.7 miles) for a 45.5 kg (100 lb) shell
Rate of fire	3 rounds/minute

A view of the gun with the breech closed.

SPECS & STATS

Crew	9
Total weight	6,200 kg (6.1 tons)
Barrel length	4.2 m (13.8 ft)
Carriage	AEC Matador artillery tractor

FACT FILE

★ Between June 1944 and May 1945, the 21st Army Group in north-west Europe fired 2,610,747 rounds of shells using 5.5 in Mk III guns.

M1 155 mm Howitzer

The M1 155 mm towed howitzer entered service with the US army in 1942 and continued to be used through both the Korean War of the 1950s and the Vietnam War of the 1960s.

It was withdrawn from US service in 1982, although it remains in use today in at least 40 countries.

▼ *In action in northern France after the Allied invasion of Europe in June 1944.*

FACT FILE

- ★ The gun was originally called the M1, but was renamed the M114 after the Second World War.
- ★ Like many big guns, the M1 had an interrupted screw breech, that is a breech with a section of its screw thread removed so that it locks quickly into the barrel.

▲ *A crew shelters the howitzer under a tree to hide it from enemy guns.*

1944

The M1 saw most action after D-Day and the invasion of Western Europe in June 1944. It was used during the capture of Cherbourg in late June and the subsequent battle for Normandy in July and August 1944.

SPECS & STATS

Crew	11
Total weight	5,600 kg (5.5 tons)
Barrel length	3.78 m (12.4 ft)
Carriage	Split-trail (two-pronged) carriage on two wheels

► *A close-up of the breech.*

ARMAMENTS

Calibre	155 mm (6.1 in)
Type of shell	High explosive
Muzzle velocity	569 m/sec (1,850 ft/sec)
Range	14.6 km (9.2 miles)
Rate of fire	40 rounds/hour

80 cm K (E) 'Schwere Gustav' Gun

The German 'Schwere Gustav' (meaning 'Heavy Gustav') gun was possibly the largest gun ever built.

It was so big that it took 25 trainloads of equipment, 1,400 men and up to six weeks to assemble. Yet it was only used for 13 days and fired a total of 48 shells.

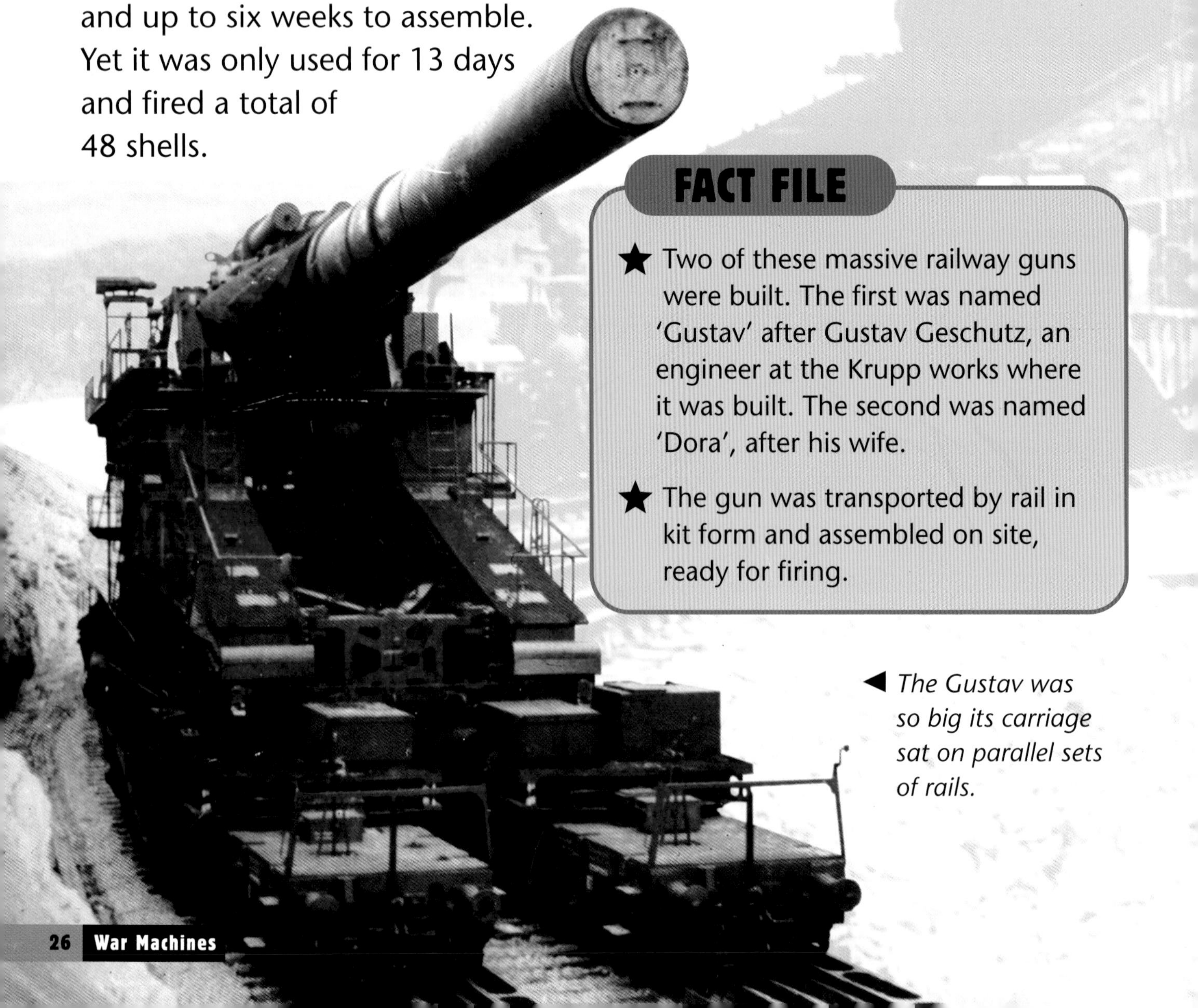

FACT FILE

- ★ Two of these massive railway guns were built. The first was named 'Gustav' after Gustav Geschutz, an engineer at the Krupp works where it was built. The second was named 'Dora', after his wife.
- ★ The gun was transported by rail in kit form and assembled on site, ready for firing.

◀ *The Gustav was so big its carriage sat on parallel sets of rails.*

SPECS & STATS

Crew	1,420 men commanded by a colonel, including 500 gunners
Weight of gun	1,365,500 kg (1,344 tons)
Barrel length	50 m (164 ft)
Carriage	Railway truck

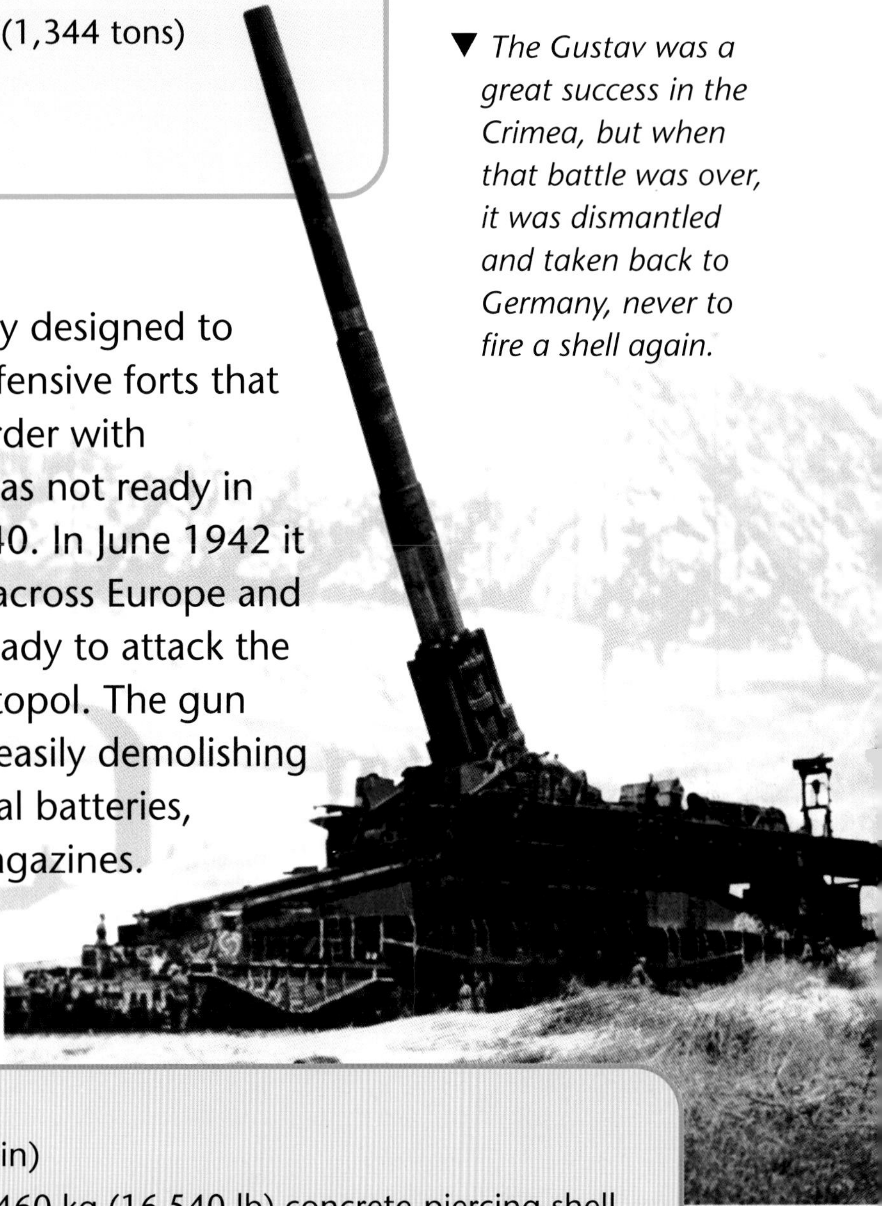

▼ *The Gustav was a great success in the Crimea, but when that battle was over, it was dismantled and taken back to Germany, never to fire a shell again.*

Attack on Sevastopol

This massive gun was originally designed to smash the Maginot Line of defensive forts that protected France's eastern border with Germany. However the gun was not ready in time for the attack in May 1940. In June 1942 it travelled along railway tracks across Europe and was installed in the Crimea, ready to attack the Soviet Black Sea port of Sevastopol. The gun proved to be a great success, easily demolishing heavily protected Soviet coastal batteries, fortresses and ammunition magazines.

ARMAMENTS

Calibre	80 cm (31.5 in)
Weight and type of shell	7,460 kg (16,540 lb) concrete-piercing shell 4,800 kg (10,584 lb) high-explosive shell
Muzzle velocity	760 m/second (2,500 ft/second)
Range	37 kg (23 miles) for concrete-piercing shell 48 km (30 miles) for high-explosive shell
Rate of fire	14 rounds/day

V-2 Rocket

The German V-2 rocket was the first man-made object ever to be sent into space and is thus the forerunner of modern space rockets.

How it worked

The V-2 consisted of a large warhead sitting on top of a powerful rocket engine that launched it up into space. After a minute, the engine cut out and the rocket flew through space before returning to Earth and hitting its target four minutes later, causing widespread death and devastation. Its flight path was controlled by an internal accelerometer that cut the engine off at the right time, thus dictating how far the rocket would fly.

Rocket trials

The first V-2 test launch took place in March 1942, but the rocket crash-landed nearby. The third test rocket was launched successfully on 3 October 1942. It flew for 193 km (120 miles) and reached a height of 80 km (50 miles), the first rocket ever to reach space. On 8 September 1944 V-2s attacked Paris and London.

► *An engineer makes adjustments to the gyroscopes that will control its stability and distance in flight.*

SPECS & STATS

Total weight	12,800 kg (28,000 lb)
Height	14.3 m (47 ft)
Speed	1,340 m/second (4,400 ft/second)
Altitude	90 km (56 miles)
Engine	Liquid-fuelled rocket engine combining 3,800 kg of fuel (75% alcohol, 25% water) with 4,900 kg of liquid oxygen
Thrust	24,950 kg (55,000 lb) at the start, increasing to 72,570 kg (160,000 lb) at maximum speed

▼ *A V-2 stands against its gantry ready for launch.*

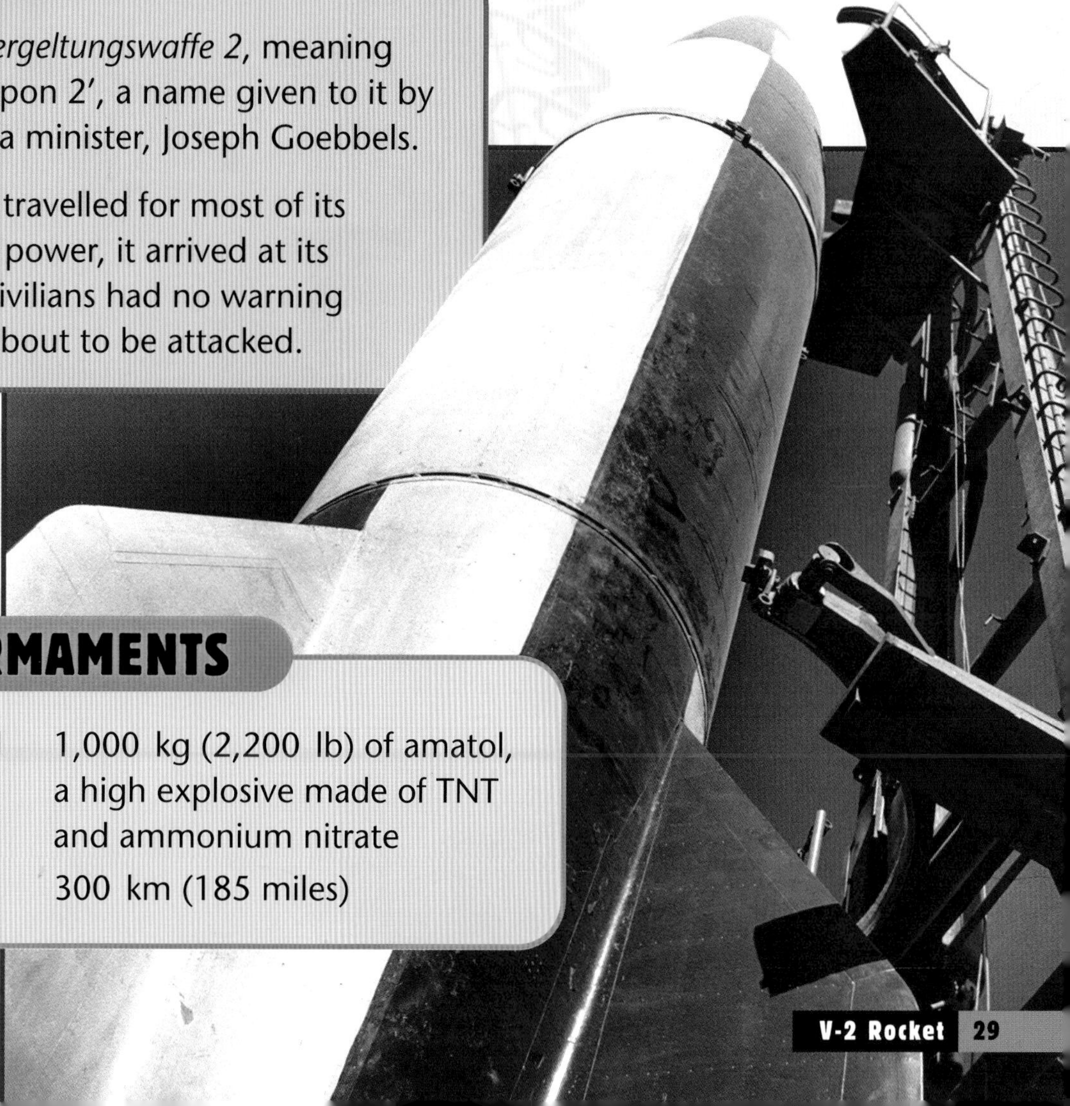

FACT FILE

★ V-2 stands for *Vergeltungswaffe 2*, meaning 'Vengeance weapon 2', a name given to it by Nazi propaganda minister, Joseph Goebbels.

★ Because the V-2 travelled for most of its journey without power, it arrived at its target silently. Civilians had no warning that they were about to be attacked.

ARMAMENTS

Warhead	1,000 kg (2,200 lb) of amatol, a high explosive made of TNT and ammonium nitrate
Range	300 km (185 miles)

Glossary

Anti-aircraft gun
A gun designed to hit enemy aircraft and bring them down.

Anti-tank gun
A powerful gun designed to pierce armour and 'kill' or knock out an enemy tank.

AP
Armour-piercing shell.

Artillery
Heavy guns pulled by horses or armoured vehicles. It can also refer to the section of the army firing the weapons.

Barrel
The long tube through which the shell is fired.

Battery
A unit of typically 6 to 8 artillery guns, grouped together to help battlefield communications and command; batteries are grouped in larger units called battalions, which are further grouped into regiments.

Breech
The opening at the end or side of the gun barrel through which the shell is inserted.

Calibre
The diameter of the bore or the inside of the barrel of a gun.

Carriage
The method by which the artillery piece is moved.

Field gun
Lightweight gun, with a bore-diameter up to about 15 cm.

Fuze
The detonator used to fire an explosive charge inside a shell.

Gun
Artillery designed to fire a high-velocity shell at a low trajectory or flight path.

Heavy gun
A heavyweight gun with a bore diameter above 20 cm.

Howitzer
Artillery designed to fire a heavy, slower shell with a high trajectory or flight-path.

hp
Horsepower, a unit of power.

Medium gun
A mediumweight gun, with a bore diameter roughly between 15 cm and 20 cm.

Mk
Short for Mark, the model or type of gun.

Muzzle velocity
The rate per second at which a shell exits the muzzle of the gun.

pdr
Short for 'pounder'.

Rate of fire
The number of shells that can be fired in a period of time.

Recoil
When a gun jumps or rolls back as a result of being fired.

Shell
A hollow artillery projectile filled with either high explosives or shrapnel and primed with a fuse to explode either during flight, on impact, or after penetration.

Shrapnel
Small pieces of metal, often metal balls, packed into a shell and designed as an anti-personnel weapon to kill or maim the enemy.

Supersonic
Flight greater than the speed of sound, which is 1235 km/h (761 mph).

Western Front
The parallel line of Allied and German trenches that ran from the English Channel south through Belgium and France to the Swiss border, and where most of the major battles of the First World War took place.

Some useful websites

The Imperial War Museum: www.iwm.org.uk/

Wikipedia entries for many of the guns in this book: type in the name of the gun in the Search box and press Go:
http://en.wikipedia.org/wiki/Main_Page

Comprehensive list of artillery on Wikipedia:
http://en.wikipedia.org/wiki/List_of_artillery

Encyclopedic sites about the two world wars:
www.spartacus.schoolnet.co.uk/FWW.htm
www.spartacus.schoolnet.co.uk/2WW.htm

BBC history sites about the two world wars:
www.bbc.co.uk/history/worldwars/wwone/
www.bbc.co.uk/history/worldwars/wwtwo/

Note to parents and teachers:
Every effort has been made by the Publishers to ensure that the websites in this book are suitable for children, that they are of the highest educational value, and that they contain no inappropriate or offensive material. However, because of the nature of the Internet, it is impossible to guarantee that the contents of these sites will not be altered. We strongly advise that Internet access is supervised by a responsible adult.

Index